The Night the Train Stopped

Janafer

Copyright 2022 Jana Jackson

Lyrics of these hymns are from
the public domain.

For the Louis Armstrong lyrics,
the author found no reasonable
way to get permission,
so she expresses thanks for the
warming effect they bring.

All artwork including cover art
was work-for-hire paid for by
Jana Jackson.

To the Memory
of
Charolette Johnson

Children of Aurio

In this flag-stop Italian town, I wondered why people, even very old people, steeped in curiosity, would come out of their shops saying in their very musical voices: *Bella Bella.* As I passed each shop the excitement seemed to grow. Perhaps it was because I was the only woman of color in this town.

*   *   *

The bulletin board in a certain university hallway had posted an opportunity to work in Italy, to be involved in how children were taught in other countries. My doctoral research had focused on interdisciplinary teaching methods with an emphasis on cultural diversity. This would be a great opportunity to observe and enjoy how children were taught in a one-culture society, that is, Italy. My acceptance astonished me. *Small-town Italy* specifically wanted me to show teachers some strategies which would enhance growth in culturally diverse classrooms.

On the morning of my arrival I found myself standing in front of Milan's gargantuan airport, praying that the interpreter would find me. I'd been told "20" for a bus to take me 140 miles to a town, the name of which I could not even pronounce. A tall Swedish woman, blonde and blue-eyed and looking out of place in a sea of Italians, held a sign, "Interpreter, Universitá dello Kansan." She spoke very little English, yet discreetly peeked into a dictionary with very small print. The 140-mile trip to her town, my final destination and summer home, went fast as we shared words and laughter, using my big picture-book dictionary, Italian and English – mine and hers – both broken. We shared stories, hand gestures and uncontrollable nods with associated laughing, as we spoke with odd accents along so many wrong paths of the words. I am from Chicago, and the second syllable "ă" of that word gave big laughs to me and to this fair-complexioned, guest-worker Swede. What a provocative and fearful way to begin the adventures for me, whereas the whole town knew I was coming. The headline that day read, "Il progetto *American University and Aurio School . . .*" as the local paper identified our project, in English.

Foschini was an elementary school for children 4th grade through 8th. Kids younger than nine years attended a school which had Montessori curricula. This school called Foschini was the type of school which had given structure to the Italian school system after World War II. A two-story building housed the Foschini School, and there were three rooms designed for those students with physical and mental challenges. Unlike in American schools, these rooms were special, distinctive, for exceptional children to receive the best possible education. Maybe things were almost reversed. In America, children with disabilities were not always given the best.

Core classes on the lower floor, music and performing arts on the upper, it was easy to find the rooms of those teachers expecting me to help design their lessons. In one large classroom, overfilled with about 25 students, to my surprise they were laughing, playing . . . dancing? I anticipated hands folded politely atop desks instead of exuberant kids. Yes, they were in festival mode so early in the morning. As I took my seat near the absent teacher's desk the students began to whisper and laugh. By experience, I started to figure out these behaviors: substitute teacher = *divertimento*, a good day for horseplay.

Students began to leave as others came in with really big smiles. The bell rang. The students began to talk so loud the announcements could not be heard. Over the loudspeakers came incomprehensible Italian, but my name was announced somewhere in a sentence with, "Be nice to the visiting teacher from America."

A few minutes after the announcements the principal walked into the room and there was an instant silence. She smiled at me and said, "Our teacher, no. Sick."

I said, "No worries. I will teach." There to teach teachers, I would just teach this class today.

To myself I chuckled that my limited Italian included "sit down/be quiet" and "priest." I sent a student with a note to telephone a certain nearby priest and ask if he'd be able to come to the classroom. Nobody knew I already had an appointment to speak with him.

As the class settled down, I began to teach math and science. Math is a universal language, and scientific jargon provides many words which sound alike. In science, instructors should emphasize prefixes and suffixes. Visiting teachers would observe how to implement cultural strategies with diverse groups. Equations in the Physics lessons use learning-style methods and techniques, even for laboratory experiments.

When the bell rang and the next class came in, the priest was standing in the door, a very large man with silver-gray hair who, with a shiny bald-spot, looked like a monk out of the 1700s. He was a holy-looking priest, his hands folded under his robe. He was Father Pouyoung from Belgium. He spoke English and Italian and several other languages. From the USA, I had contacted him, knowing my job would be difficult due to the diversity. These students came from many countries. My job would be to teach the teachers, and for me it was a privilege to work with culturally diverse students.

As this second class entered the room, the sound of talking and laughter stopped. As if the noise hit a wall without bouncing back, the silence embraced a totally different environment. The kids greeted Father Pouyoung and then me, their teacher for the day. "Hello, Monsignor," in English: how touching because up to this point they'd led me to believe they spoke only Italian.

Later that day I was told the school was up for reevaluation, from England, seeking eighty-percent proficiency. I was told that students were saying there was a new sheriff in town from the USA, who'd deputized a priest. Her name was Miss Beatrice and she was most definitely a teacher who knew about classroom management.

Walking the Town

Built in a circle, railroad tracks at the end of the town, those homes of the 1700s stopped at the railroad tracks, there where the vineyards started. There was one major street, the only straight one, which led to the north or to the south. Not having cross streets was so different for a girl raised in big-city Chicago. It was hard to get lost so long as you stayed on the path, in a circle, knowing you'd cross over the straight street halfway through your walk. There was a great and picturesque fountain in the center of Aurio.

As the days went by Miss Beatrice's Italian grew stronger but her students still enjoyed teasing her in English because it was easier for them to do that than for her to stumble around in a language where she could not master the sounds. To listen to the students speak was like listening to music all day long. Their voices carried different tones but she could tell who was speaking by the song sung. I taught math and science using Rita Dunn's learning-style methods, so there was academic growth, using English, not only in my own class but in other classes. The students assimilated fine, as boys picked on girls and prim girls took it without giving it back. In little time they were designing puzzles and learning-task cards, along with Thinking Maps which were Rita's creation. "Miss Bea" introduced teaching tools which took off all over the school. Studying English in many subjects, along with the visits from Monsignor, transformed that classroom into a wonderful world. I almost forgot I was just a substitute, not paid for my efforts except by room and board. Yet how could anyone place a value on a gracious family's home, aromatic food, the rich red color of wine, to sleep in a room designed for a princess, marble floors and all.

At school everyone seemed to disappear at the end of the day. In my host family the husband owned and ran a pharmacy, and his remarkable wife had a shop for medicinal herbs. Working ended later than school, so I had no ride home. Others offered to drive me to the marble-floored castle, but being there alone was not appealing. So walking the town became a nice option. There was a florist's shop from which arose fresh-flower smells, as if honey and lilacs, which brought me to walk that way.

There were many shops on this path and lots of people who began to come out of their shops, and with smiles, sometimes with tears, saying *Bella Bea Bella* as I walked. That's the Italian word for *beautiful.* Sometimes I'd go into the shops to find people waiting with flowers and candy, offering me hot baked bread fresh from the oven, with olive oil and wine. Gesturing for me to sit down to eat and drink, they'd smile like my grandmother, Big Momma, as she'd sit me down to eat cornbread muffins straight out of the oven, cutting them in half to add grape jam mixed with melting butter, oozing from the sides. She'd watch me gobble them down with milk, with the same smile these Italians had, watching me gobble down *pasticcini* with wine.

They offered gifts of whatever was in the shop, but I sought to humble myself. "Please let me not take from you." They'd shake their heads as the young ones translated. In this town, it would be unkind not to accept what might be offered – it's their way.

To avoid so much attention I wished I could just stay at school and not see those shopkeepers. By now the whole town knew how I'd route my everyday, afternoon walk. They enjoyed the shop stops. If I didn't show up they'd send their grandchildren to school to make sure I was alright. So I began to choose a different path each day. Quietly listening, I could meet, greet and speak with everyone. Regardless of where I might start, I always ended up by the center-of-town fountain. It didn't take long before everyone knew the African-American teacher, and it was humbling to know they were waiting for Bella Bea Bella to grace their shops. This routine seemed to make the elders happiest.

The daily receiving of gifts brought back so many memories of times spent in the summer, writing, with my grandmother. She'd have me write thank-you cards in response to compliments on my singing from Louisiana church members. Now I was learning to write and spell in Italian, "Thank you for your gift," while wishing I had something to give other than just a card.

To visit Father Pouyoung, one afternoon I decided to take the path that led past the church. It was time for an update on student behaviors, and I could ask him for help in figuring out the best answer to this challenge: how to give back in an Italian way. "They love me a lot!" How to repay such heartfelt kindness was genuinely difficult, so different from my past experiences. The elders in this Italian town cried tears of joy and I did not understand why. I asked the Father why these people liked me so much. It was not the young ones, whom I taught daily, but their grandparents, elders, and some of them used walkers – little tennis balls and all – to greet me. Some walked with canes, yet touched my face with both hands, eyes showing feelings I could not comprehend. Hands clasping warmly, squeezing my cheeks and speaking in their musical, harmonic voices, there was something bewildering about the greetings.

Be it known, talking with Father was like walking the town – he spoke in circles. The question you'd start with was the place you'd finish. Father looked at me and shook his head, "My dear little one, breathe. What is not to like about you? You're delightful." For these Italian elders I must have represented the Americans of the last war. In a mysterious way, compassion of the past was coming through.

* * *

This particular day, down one little street, incredible guitar music was filling the air with a classical beat, a mixture of jazz and Spanish melodies. How strange to hear such good, old-fashioned, New Orleans jazz, in a town which edified nothing other than one hundred percent Italian customs. The louder the guitar got, the more intricate the notes sounded. I began to think of my dad playing music with his friends B. B. King and Sonny Stitt, who blew his tenor, while Dad played his baritone saxophone. Mister B. B. on his guitar was magical because the strings sounded like the many voices singing in our church choir. As I walked closer to the apartment where the music originated, the sounds created a vision of my mom bringing ice-cold lemonade topped with Uncle Nokomi's fresh mint leaves from the garden which he planted in the backyard of our Chicago home. As I walked toward this Louisiana jazz, coming from nimble Italian fingers, I tried to sing, making up words, and people smiled. I reached down low, scatting basso tones as I invented words. Maybe . . . I was not the only person of color in this town?

As I approached the apartment building, I saw the music was coming from an open window, and I could feel the vibrations of the strings. Sitting on the stairs, I closed my eyes and yes, the real words came to my mind. Then, what! The music changed from jazz to classical – no lead into it, no pause, the music changed from jazz to classical. Were there two different musicians?

It was time to continue the walk toward my rendezvous where the host-family car would take me to the castle. The populous street was a charming choice, store vendors coming out to shake my hand or speak words I didn't understand. People now were looking out the windows. Women had their heads wrapped in that classic traditional style and the burgundy or tan-brown kerchiefs contrasted nicely with their aprons.

After the car ride home, my chores began. The chores got simple when I learned how to fix Italian salad. In this town people did not go to the store all the time, but instead they planted lush red-, yellow- and green-gardens for salad. I had volunteered to contribute, sharing dinner the first time, by gathering combinations from the garden. In my Chicago family, as a woman, I'd been expected to cook, but here I didn't know how. So, in broken Italian, I explained how Mom would not allow anyone into her kitchen while she cooked. Mostly my job was to clean our Chicago home and iron the clothes. These hosts, with their multi-colored gardens, understood, so the salad in this instance gave me a great opportunity.

For at least a half-hour I looked through the refrigerator to find something to make the salad with. Then the youngest child, Stefano, pulled on my dress and took me outside to the garden. I could see the others staring passionately and grinning wholeheartedly. Yes, American woman, *not even able to fix a salad* was written all over their faces. Stefano pointed to the garden and I almost passed out: I was from Chicago, the inner city, where nothing grew in the concrete. That was where Jane Byrne delivered lemons for lemonade to the poor people, yet, they had no sugar. Then she ran for mayor of Chicago . . . and so the story goes. You cannot make a salad from what I'd seen in the concrete jungle.

It's hard to create something, with little knowledge, from nothing. How could you fix a salad from vegetables growing in a garden? Stefano, not but six years old, began to pull up this green stuff. It was certainly not iceberg. So I started to . . . and, oh no, slugs on the green stuff! Okay. Now people were crossing the road, so the laughter was getting louder and louder. Even the dogs were excited. Cats skedaddled from the windows. This is not going to end well.

Stefano's mouth was open, he giggled so hard, and now even I was laughing. How funny is this? Slugs in the garden. When I stood up from my cucumber picking, people of all ages were there talking with each other. They gathered tomatoes, oh yes, strawberries and yellow peppers. Some were wiping their eyes from tears of laughter.

Stefano was pulling my dress to get me to go back inside. Now the people from across the road got busy. Older women were washing off the slugs and talking. They showed me how to put the green stuff in a spinning bowl to separate the slugs from the Italian lettuce, without mashing the slugs. There was such an abundance – they brought things from across the road, and the cutting and the shearing and the amount of food was incredible. They began to cook and talk and bring more food, then the books came out: old recipe books and more talking. Hours later, what a feast! Everyone was ready to eat. So many people under the vine canopy – it faced the road. More plates got added to the table with bottles of wine, the men comparing the family labels. Then silence, stillness, and they prayed in Italian. Out of nowhere, the table was set in a fine way, and the food appeared like magic. It was so well planned, plates and food materialized at the same time. As they passed dishes around, it was hard to know which one you had placed on your plate. Conversations in that rich language accented the rich-wine aroma. And Stefano and I smiled, knowing our salad was the best!

The next day I got to class early and wanting to try out one of my teaching strategies, thinking it was time for the students to learn the English versions of the science words. I would be able to teach faster and the students would become more adept with the content. I had asked Father Pouyoung to come in the afternoon just in case his support was needed. Sometimes the boys just did not want to learn and I knew that seeing his white clerical collar, with his long black robe, would stop the playing.

Flashcard was the word of the day and drilling the English was one way to get the science- and math-concepts taught. A few weeks later it would be announced the school was to participate in the International Language Test for British English, which is different from American English. The Task Cards, versions of flashcards, which I'd studied in Dr. Rita Dunn's New York City workshop, were paying off as I passed her learning strategy on to these Italian and African students. They enjoyed my teacher-modeling, which worked well in Art class also. The students were to imagine words of Italian, or of African dialect, as reminder words. They'd visualize a picture of a sentence. Hot pasta in the mouth was one of my best.

To everyone's amazement the school passed the test. A few misplaced parts of speech, British versus American, occurred. Apparently, the only words missed were British jargon. As the tester left the building she stopped by my classroom and said,

"Next time try using British words." She smiled with a sort of delight that the entire school had passed. This was a first: an accomplishment long overdue.

As the second British examiner passed me on his way out, a half-grin on his face, he said, "Oh well, passing is passing."

Wonderful World

I had grown accustomed now to going by the open apartment window, music in the air, and sitting on the stairs that led up to the flat. A very handsome man often stood there. Music flowed like cotton candy, attaching its sugary cloud to the paper cone as it whirled around, getting bigger and bigger. I sat there relaxing, moving gently to the music. One day I heard a particularly talented guitar rendition of "What a Wonderful World." Although I didn't know the words, I knew the tune so I began to sing with runs of jazz. That's the way I'd learned as my dad played baritone sax in our backyard in Chicago. Yes, this guitar music took my mind to Dad and B. B. King. And my voice echoed through the air. My soul swayed to the music and my voice, from deep tones to high, skipped through those runs. I made up the words, but who could care? No one was out there to hear me. Except — they really were listening. Everyone was listening and they came out, especially at the end. The clapping was a little embarrassing.

In gratitude, I bowed to everyone who'd come out, throwing a small kiss, humbly respectful. Something incredible happened. There in the window stood a very young child with a guitar strapped to his shoulder. Why, it was little Noah, the blind boy! I would notice him, reading in braille, every day as I went to my teaching assignment. Music, of a man, accomplished – coming from a child. Soulful jazz flowed from a classical guitar. This is a wonderful world.

*I see trees of green,
Red roses too,
A bright, blessed day,
Clouds pink, sky blue.
I think to myself :
What a wonderful world.*

The handsome man on the stairs was Noah's father. He appeared at the door and invited me up. It had been a long walk, so what a relief. Blind Noah's smile gave away that he knew who I was. "Miss Bea, your perfume smells good," he said.

Each morning I would mix two different perfumes to make the fragrance my own, but I'd never realized the deep meaning of distinctive until then.

The apartment was a modest one. I could see the difference between the marbled-floor castle where I was staying, vine-laced canopy and all, contrasted with this little kitchen designed for two.

Noah's father began to tell the story of his son born blind and a mother who died when he was little. Teaching blind children there in Italy was very different from America's educational system. Italian children with special challenges were treated with far more respect, and rightfully so. Everything in the school surrounded their needs, even the designs of the classroom, the restroom.

The townspeople loved all children and they showed their love through the care given to those with challenges. Noah was the protégé of a world-renowned tenor and was following in his footsteps. Noah's guitar playing mimicked the tenor's singing: such great genius twice from the same small town.

Noah's father dropped the pasta into the pot of boiling water. The smell of fresh bread flowed through the window. Soon afterward, knocks on the door began, and the food and people began to pour in. The aromas flowed. Salad was fresh and clean with no slugs. Mmmmm, tiramisu pudding. Wine, tasting of old cork, dark red with the family label written in pencil, with an oaken deepness.

Yes, it was time to eat and enjoy family talk. The room filled with conversations. Children laughed as people sat in the stairs – oh, everywhere – eating. Fresh flowers adorned the tables: the kitchen table, the credenza, lamp tables in the corners. It was a pasta feast and even when you couldn't eat any more, more was mysteriously added to your plate. And then came the parade of desserts. Every dessert was, as required by custom, to be tasted. The more you gave compliments, the more got served, which meant more for you to eat. Everybody had to be complimented, especially the grandmothers, who cooked from their mothers' recipes. It didn't take me much effort to give compliments: everything was the best I'd ever tasted. As long as my own grandmother didn't come through that door, well, I was safe.

As the sun began to go down, people gathered around Noah's grandfather, who was the oldest of the old. Then, I heard the story – it was for me. Noah's grandfather began.

The Story

"The night-a, she was cold. I was the one to go gather coal from the train tracks. There was always coal left on the tracks from the German train – it took coal to the camps where they held the

Jews. Always enough to carry home to Uncle where we piled it next to the old black stove, hopefully enough to keep us warm for many nights. To pick up coal was my job, coal for our family, and Uncle would give away coal to the older people who had no kids to gather it for them. Everybody would stay warm; the winter nights were cold in our part of the town where Jewish people chose to live together.

"That night, after making a great fire in the black stove, we went to the woods. That was where Uncle and I would gather dry vines from a vineyard to add to our hidey-hole. He had hollowed out a staircase around the roots. Each night we would dig deeper and deeper under the tree. I would spend my nights in the hole in case the train should stop in our town, looking for Jewish people to put into the camps.

"As a boy I knew. I knew what to do if the train stopped and soldiers got off the train ready to imprison us. My uncle told me many times what the solders would do if they caught us. Uncle would say, 'Hiding, not enough. The journey is just starting.'

"It would be my job to share this journey with my grandchildren in the future. It was important not to forget the journey. If the train should stop, then I was to hide and focus on staying alive no matter what happened outside the hidey-hole. Staying put, staying quiet, staying alive by sleeping in the day and coming out only at night until the soldiers boarded the train to go away.

"**Vines along** the train rails needed to stay put. But the vines near to the woods would be the best ones to build a nest and lace between the tree roots that stuck out in the hole. We brought stuffing from the blankets Auntie would use making her quilts and we lined the nest where I would sleep. Sometimes when out in the woods we could hear gunshots in the distance. Uncle would tell me to get as many vines as I could carry and run deep in the woods. Somehow Uncle knew how far away the sounds traveled. Only, once he told me to run home, not look back, and Uncle almost beat me running. I didn't know he could run like that.

"**Almost all** the Jews lived in the ghetto area. When the war started my parents had sent me to live with my uncle and aunt. They said it would be safer. Jews disappeared nightly, and ours was the last stop before crossing the Austrian border, and that was probably why the train passed this stop every night.

"**The town** was split into two sections. The Catholics lived on one side of the town and the Jews on the opposite. Our temple was located at one end of the town and the Catholic church was at the other. I think they were built around the same time and they tried to outdo each other with the height of the towers, but both were pretty high.

"The fountain in the center faced the monastery library, built hundreds of years before the town was developed. There, the pope kept books, important papers, gold and things of value that belonged to the church. The local rabbi and the local priest would walk from either end of town to use this library. They prepared messages for the people.

"Many townspeople studied, using books in the library that dated back to before Christ. Great religious times in Italy. The town was a peaceful place. Most people kept to themselves except when it was time for weddings or funerals. They seemed to respect everyone's customs.

"It was a nice town but Uncle would tell me every day, 'If the Germans come, do not share your hidey-hole with anyone. Just jump in, cover yourself and stay quiet.' My aunt would bake bread and wrap cheese and put it in a knapsack near the fireplace every night. This was my food, perhaps for a long time, so I needed to eat small pieces. There was a jug of water with a little wine mixed in so the flavor would not spoil. After prayers, I would recite to Uncle the plan, not leaving out any details: get my food and water-wine, go down the fireplace stairs, staying clear of the wall, hot from the fireplace. Get to the bottom, crawl out of the little window to my hiding place, do not look back. Crawl quietly into my hidey-hole and pull down the pinecone-and-vines top. Uncle built that with Auntie's quilt stuffing.

"Using the vine-laced roots to lower myself into the hole, covering each root with vines Uncle had left for me. The design was simple. He made two roofs, so somebody falling on the first one would not fall on me but on top of the second roof which was stronger.

"As I completed repeating all the instructions for a journey of night terrors, I looked upon Uncle's face. What great pain shone in his blue-gray eyes. These were the same eyes I'd seen in my mother that last time. These were the same eyes as mine, so much sadness if this journey happened: so many days of planning, so many nights of quiet torment for a just-in-case-the-train-stops.

"I went to bed angry and upset! To lose my mom and dad, and to think of losing Uncle and Auntie. Upset and with tears I slept on a wet pillow listening for a train I prayed would never come. We prayed every night the train would not stop and the soldiers would not come to our little town. We prayed the nightmare of the Jews would not touch this town, the way the night terror touched so many . . . not understanding: why the Jews? *It will not come to pass* haunted my thoughts as my eyes closed into a restless sleep."

Sparrow's Eyes

As we sat on the stairs leading up to Noah's apartment, people gathered: in the small kitchen, in the little room that faced the sunset where two loveseats faced each other, in chairs next to two end-tables, in Noah's room where his guitar sat alongside a chair by his window. People from the neighborhood sat and stood all over. No matter how many times Grandfather's story got told, all were touched so deeply. Noah walked into his room, reached for his guitar and searched for the sounds in the room, using his sixth sense. There stood Noah, guitar in hand, in the doorway from his bedroom to the sitting room.

"Bea, sing for us," Noah said, as the chatter diminished. Noah always knew me by my perfume blend, and I liked the way he called my name. "Bea, sing those songs the Negroes sang, the black soldiers who buried those kids back in World War Two."

"I don't sing Italian, Noah," I said.

His smile was so wide it could have jumped off his face, as he said, "They don't speak English!"

Noah began to play my Big Momma's favorite song as everyone gathered around Grandfather to hear of that night the train stopped.

"Do you know other songs?" Noah asked me.

My head bowed, my eyes focused on him, I said, "Only church songs." It was so easy to remember the music and the sound of voices in the church, but not all the words. Sometimes I'd just make up the words.

The music came from Noah's guitar in such rich tones both high and low. Regardless of where the range would go, he matched the sounds with great passion. The guitar chords flowed magically, making the melody so easy to sing. Noah played with joy, soulfully. How amazing it was to see his closed eyes moving, his head swaying in all directions, exaggeratedly.

With every tone Noah saw visions of notes we could only hear. As the rhythms began to touch my heart, I had thoughts of Louisiana, of following Big Momma up the hill to church on Sunday morning. She and I would hear voices of praise flowing from the church, welcoming us as we entered the place where worship and song blended together. Honoring God, so early on a Louisiana Sunday morning.

Hearing the melody from Noah's guitar, of the song that came out from my soul, I sang:

Why should I feel discouraged?
Why should the shadow come?
Why should my heart be lonely?
And long for heavenly home.

I began to move around the room and touch those who were listening so intently.

When Jesus is my portion,
My constant friend is He . . .

I could see in their eyes certain love, and I felt warmth of spirit.

. . . His eye is on the sparrow,
And I know He watches me.

Turning around, touching everyone's eyes, singing stronger, controlling my pitch to match each chord from Noah's guitar. I sang with strength like Big Momma.

For His eye is on the sparrow,
And I know God watches me.

Tears now formed in their eyes and ran down their faces.

I sing because I am happy,
Oh yes, I sing because I am free.
For His eyes are on the sparrow,
And I know God watches me.

Grandfather had told us about living in the town, people greeting each other every day. What excitement in his voice as he'd described the homes and the shops and the churches and the schools. But we could tell: Grandfather was weary. He was one of the oldest members in the temple and could only tell his story in parts. I wanted to be in the chair beside Grandfather to hear the next part of his story.

I see skies of blue and clouds of white,
The bright blessed day, the dark sacred night,
And I think to myself: what a wonderful world.

The sun was beginning to set and it was time for Noah's father to take me home. The little roads did not have streetlights and few people had cars with headlights, so that meant no headlights to show where the winding road was going. As we drove home I hummed the tunes, following note by note Noah's guitar which I could hear in my mind's ear. These songs were full of the plans made by slaves who ran away from the plantation, praying to be freed men and freed women. They had visions of either a new life or a heavenly home with Jesus. This was a wonderful, magical night – it is indeed a wonderful world.

Hush, hush, somebody calling my name,
Oh my Lord, oh my Lord, what shall I do?

The next day at school everyone knew I had sung at Noah's house. News traveled really fast in this little town. Singing, for me, was humbling because my mere voice was nothing compared to his incredible playing. Perhaps, because people would hear him play the guitar so often at school and in social gatherings, they did not realize how powerful his music was. And blind, and age twelve.

Noah's mother died when he was four. His visions of her were from the memories he held in his fingers of caressing her face. Noah's father was still a young man at that time. No one really knew what was going on inside Noah's head at age four, but his behaviors in school said he needed help reaching out to others. He'd just given up on everything.

One day his teacher came to class with an old guitar and Noah smiled for the first time in a long time. He began to light up his world and everyone around him. His guitar became a part of him. Water sprang from his fountain, carving out a special place, still and peaceful waters. No one knew his gift would inspire a whole town.

*   *   *

Grandfather's storytelling and Noah's music contrasted with schooldays in this fourth- through eighth-grade setting. Days, classic days of school. Science terminology on flash puzzle-cards, my favorite students being themselves, showing animated drama. But today there would be some surprises for my students.

The town priest and rabbi would visit the classes in the afternoon, after lunch when behaviors reached their peak! Well the students would begin to understand "*Basta*, *basta*." "Enough is enough," enough playful behavior in our science assignments. The students showed misbehavior often, but they were not mean-spirited, just full of fun.

The goal this year was for all students to pass the English test on science and mathematics words. Definitions were displayed on those puzzle cards. They'd had to write their answers, in English, for those examiners from England.

As the stress of the day got higher and higher, I longed for the peace of Noah's music flowing from his window as I walked the town after each day in school. There was something different about the music coming from the choir room before school. It always began with voice exercises and practice songs. Today the student voices sang Negro spiritual words, but with a twist of Catholic-Italian.

How could they change the music so much? The richness of the students' harmony was unbelievable, but the words just did not fit those Negro spirituals of my childhood memories.

So, during my planning period I went to the room and asked the music teacher if she would like me to sing one of the songs the way we sang it in the little church on the hill. Singing the song without the piano brought back so many good memories, practicing with Big Momma and Mama Jack for my Sunday solos. As this teacher began to play her piano, the music came back to me, flowing with richness.

I sing because I am happy,
I sing because I am free,
For His eyes are on the sparrow,
And I know God watches me.

My great-grandmother, Mama Jack, lived in Louisiana near the Mississippi River where the songs were deep in soulful memories of slavery.

It was fun changing the songs and the beats to match the music, to match how they were sung in church. I also remembered the downside of going to church, practicing those solo songs so early in the morning when the sun was just peeking over the hill. Big Momma would carry her basket of biscuits and hot fried chicken, green beans, and the one which is still my favorite side-food, sweet candied yams. She sang in a very deep tone while Mama Jack carried the high pitch, harmonizing the two voices. And Mama Jack always toted her basket of desserts, hot peach and apple pies and the almond pound cake dusted with powdered sugar which melted in your mouth. Oh, yes, no need to chew, because that would take away the flavor. All day Saturday they would prepare foods for church and I, as a child, would spend that day dreaming of eating fried chicken . . . with sweets!

Students carried over English-language skills to other classes. My university professors would be proud, as was I. These kids now used English in every subject, in every classroom and even at home. All these experiences, including visits from priest and rabbi, gave birth to my mental impressions, weaving patterns to last.

Oh my gosh, distracted, I almost forgot this was the morning planning period. Hearing my name on that annoying loudspeaker, I began running to get to my classroom. Singing with the music teacher had brought back so many memories. But a busy mind makes the day go faster.

Star of David

The grander map around Aurio composed six paths leading in six different directions to form a Star of David. From the town square one path led to the railroad platform and from there the daily train, during the war and in modern times, traveled to Austria. There was a large fountain in the center of town, and every Saturday was an open market where shopkeepers, seamstresses, winemakers and farmers traded and sold their goods. There was lots of room for bikes and cars to park. Most people walked from far and near to visit in the morning hours, to drink coffee on benches or around small tables near the fountain. As a guest in town it was a joy to have such a simple system of roads, multiple choices of which way to go. After school, my host family would pick me up and take me home and I did not want to be late. On these daily walks, I'd say *buon giorno* to parents, grandparents and great-grandparents as I passed their homes. Street sweepers, merchants or vendors selling their wares . . . enjoying time until my host family came. The star-road layout really helped a person – well, a tuned-in person – find the right way. This was so different from Big Momma's roads which just went two ways to and from town. In Louisiana, you didn't get lost just staying on the same straight road. Here, a fountain and a star.

People came out of their shops. They'd wave, always chanting *Bella Bea Bella*. It was just like walking the straight road from Big Momma's house up the hill to church, greeting Louisiana folks sitting on their porches.

That uphill walk to church was in the early morning, but it was hot. As a little girl, I never told Big Momma, while she rubbed my legs and arms with cooking grease, how it felt to be larded up. She had a can of lard mixed with something that smelled like roses and she called it grease but I knew it as lard. It would keep my skin from drying, from turning a grayish ash color which she called *ashee*. She walked me uphill perspiring at 7 o'clock in the morning. "Baby, don't wanna be ashy when you sing your solo. Come here baby," she would say, "we need to get that 'ashy' off you before church." Oh yes, getting the ash color off required cooking me like fried chicken. You could've fried an egg in that dirt. What a laugh, the sight of me rubbing my legs together to stop the lard from running into my socks. And shoes stuck to socks all day long. This gave new meaning to hot, fried dark-meat when thinking about the chicken in Big Momma's basket.

It was a real relief to get into that tiny church, to cool off before my solo. Singing, swaying, clapping, socks sticking with lard to the inside of my shoes. I had a firsthand experience of what the chickens must have felt going from the flour coating into the frying pan.

Smells bring back memories. Big Momma and Mama Jack cooked Sunday breakfast and prepared church supper at the same time. Fresh eggs came from the henhouse, out the back door. Sourdough biscuits got made from milk which they'd set on the windowsill to sour with the sunrise. They knew how long to let the dough sit before kneading it, and here I was surrounded by *pasta di meliga*, cornmeal cookies. Back then, Big Momma never had to wake me up; the smell of bacon frying did that. The milk would warm near that old white gas-stove, which was boiling eggs to make stuffed eggs for church supper. My family would laugh at me because I was skinny but could have eggs and biscuits and bacon, and still eat a fried-chicken dinner plus almond cake.

Mama Jack, my great-grandmother, was raised by her grandmother, who was a slave from Africa, bought and sold in the New Orleans slave trade. When the slaves were freed, Mama Jack's mother left behind her three-month-old baby girl, Salina Mae, promising to return after preparing a better life in the North. But she never came back. Mama Jack was raised to be a respectful Negro girl who could cook, iron clothes and clean a house from top to bottom. These skills, by her grandmother's plan, assured her being hired in White people's homes, in that Louisiana small town. She was raised <u>not</u> to work picking cotton, and at age sixteen she went to work as hired help; her grandmother's plan worked. She saved her money and purchased property where she planted cotton on the edge of town – for others to pick. While people worked her land she grew cucumbers, pickled them, took them to New Orleans to sell in the shops with labels of her own design. Yes, she worked so hard for family that her savings put her granddaughter, my Aunt Odell, through a Negro college where she became the first teacher in our family, making me the second. Mama Jack's only child was my grandfather, my *Daddy's* father, and Daddy's sister was Aunt Odell.

Life in Louisiana was not like home in Chicago, and I grew up with both. In Chicago, Mom would buy a can of biscuits from the store and pop the can a few times until it opened – or didn't, making her bang and bang and bang. Nope, not sourdough biscuits. Down South, the kitchen had two angels singing in it. They sang as they cooked, voices blending so well. Perhaps this is why I sing both the high and the low in my Sunday songs: love of song inspired by the Holy Spirit.

Jesus loves me . . . this I know,

For the Bible tells me so.
Little ones to God belong,
They are weak but He is strong.

My tears always form when singing this song. Big story, few words, major journey trusting in the written word.

Yes, Jesus loves me,
Yes, Jesus loves me,
Yes, Jesus loves me,
For the Bible tells me so.

Walking up the Louisiana hill you could hear the voices of praise from the little church that sat on top. The older people sang and blessed every inch of the church before Sunday School would begin. The words were simply in the hymnals, but soulful music defined the arrangements which never came out as written. They all took turns singing the lead. I wondered how they switched the lead parts: not a look, not a nod toward each other. They sang their own versions but still maintained a balance in melody. What soulful blends, tones harmonizing the lows and the highs.

Sometimes I feel like a motherless child,
Sometimes I feel like a motherless child,
Sometimes I feel like a motherless child,
A long way from home.

This song brought revelation into Mama Jack's eyes. It was because of her mother's not coming back to get her. Someone would always take the lead, "A long way from home," passing the lead around. Nobody directed them, yet no one tripped over the lead; it all was spirit-felt.

Now, from the Italian choir room, I heard the voices filling the hall with old, Negro spirituals. I walked toward it. The students sang many a variation of the same song. As I approached the choir room, Big Momma's and Mama Jack's voices invaded my thoughts, and my mind could hear melodies they'd sung. Oh how they'd brought spirituality into it all. Remembering that Louisiana church, the pianist playing chords for me to find the right notes, me singing *a cappella*.

To the Italian choir-teacher I explained how my voice was not anything but just a voice. After she gave permission, I began to sing the low octaves and then the high, mixing, emulating the voices of the past. I sang Mama Jack's parts as I held back emotion, not because of remembering any stories about her mother and slavery, but because I could see her eyes. I could imagine the way she would have moved, singing for her grandmother, the African slave, and now for her son, my grandfather. Big Momma and my grandfather got married as the first World War was coming to an end. Mama Jack often sang for me at night after we prayed, and surely the way she sang for me was the way her slave-grandmother had sung for her. Her rosewater perfume – the wind blew through the open window. She pulled the sheets close to my chin. She kissed my forehead before I fell asleep.

Oh Lord, a long way from home,
A long way from home.
Sometimes I feel like a motherless child
Longing for Mama to come home.

Do believe,
Do believe, Lord,
Longing for Mama to come home.

Walking Accompaniment

There was a flower shop near the school that carried a smell of roses and mixed flowers. The Italian language just sounds like pretty flowers, but I just can't recall the names of these shops, these shops on the path leading to the fountain. The townspeople would gesture for me to sit as they carried out sweet-bread puddings and tiramisu and hot tea. Their smiles were just like my grandmother's when she served me almond cake and warm milk, standing up and watching me as I ate.

The walk often took longer than expected. One day as I got to the end of the path and entered the circle of shops, there came a sudden hush which startled me. It created a tingling deep in my stomach. Hush, Lord, somebody's calling your name. It just flowed out of my mouth as if that were the next song on a playlist.

*Hush, Lord, somebody's calling your name.
Oh my Lord, oh my Lord, what shall I do?*

Clueless, I continued to walk and Noah's music was suddenly behind me. He began to play – somehow he knew this *What shall I do?* song. Noah stayed upon the dirt path as if he could see, strumming chords to a song he didn't know. How amazing that he could walk without any red-tipped white stick. He was soon next to me beating the rhythms of the song on his guitar. We walked, making up words and chords as tingling feelings got swapped for songs and laughter. I said, "Hey, by the way, where did you come from?"

"I came from school," Noah said with a smile in his voice. "I walk this way past the shops every day. I circle, waiting for my father. Hey, did you know our apartment is down this road?"

The next day my classroom was extra full of music students: thirty students, twenty desks. Perhaps the day before I'd sung so loud – a little too much? – and now more than music students filled the room. People not only were sitting in the desks and on the desks, but they were standing all around the walls. One student said with a loud voice, "We are here to take you to the choir room. Sing your grandmother's songs for us."

Out of my mouth jumped the same songs Noah had accompanied me on while walking. To myself, I wondered which? The songs of slavery, or the ones we had fun making up?

When we reached the music room, it was filled with people from town, schoolteachers, even the principal. Some stood on risers near the door, others were along the walls, every chair was full. There were shopkeepers, grandparents, even the woman who cleaned the rooms after school, all waiting to hear those songs of slavery. What an honor. Why so much interest? My singing wasn't <u>that</u> good. It was just those old Negro songs sung differently.

And, there next to the piano sat Noah, on a stool, and with the biggest grin. I asked, "Did you know about this yesterday? Was it planned?" Noah's joyful face gave the answer away.

*   *   *

On my way to the fountain in the center of town, evening time, I took the path through Noah's neighborhood. The stairs to his apartment were full of neighbors. Oh yes, *Bella Bea Bella* and claps resounded around the neighborhood which was not that large, so the echoing sounded louder than the thirty-or-so people outside waiting for me. They began to open a space for me which led up the apartment stairs.

So this made one of the top two most embarrassing moments of my life. The other had been getting caught on camera, big eyes plus a wide grin, teasing boys at age six. Our pastor took the snapshot, and it got published in the church bulletin. In fact, it got framed and displayed all over the place, and my father, without words, made me feel like my fingers had been caught in the cookie jar.

This experience in Italy was overwhelming in a similar way. Humbling. How to thank everyone for so much kindness, how to repay their endearing love?

The Night the Train Stopped

When Noah's father saw me approaching the apartment he came down the stairs quickly. He gestured for me to come inside. As I walked up the stairs the sounds of voices were almost at a whisper. Are they waiting for me? In the middle of the room sat the oldest person of the town, Noah's grandfather, ready to continue his story about that night.

"**It was cold** that night so gathering up dried vines from the vineyard needed to be quick. The night air was so cold – I just didn't want to stay out in the cold. I longed to be near the fire which Uncle was building right before I left the warmth of our home. The fire, hot by now, with fresh-vine smell mixed with Auntie's sweet-hot-chocolate aroma; Auntie had that waiting for me every night after doing my chores.

"**This night** was somehow different. There was a tingling feeling of fear which tightened the back of my neck. Perhaps it was due to the cold. Perhaps I was thinking too much about how a train might stop instead of rattling on down the track. Usually the coal we needed just fell off. Easily I could see the ebony coal glimmering in the moonlight.

"**The train** generally would not stop, passing by our little town. My every heartbeat throbbed in my ears. And the train approached then passed our stop. Safe. What a relief. Fear began to run in my veins, sending blood faster into my head. I heard the train wheels squeal as they reversed, picking up speed, coming back, backing up! This was the last stop in Italy before Austria. Oh God, no, it's backing up.

"**Auntie and Uncle** were at home waiting for me to bring in the coal and vines for the fire. But the drill, the procedure for the event any train may stop, was for me to go straight to the hidey-hole. 'If the Nazi train stops at our town, work your way down into the hidey-hole.' I visualized Uncle's hand on my shoulder, 'Have courage.'

"**My feet,** they were stuck to the ground. I could not move. Wind pushed my body forward as tears ran down my face changing to patches of ice crystals. My body got stiff, so full of fear. Where do I go? Thinking of family, I ran toward Auntie's and Uncle's apartment in the ghetto.

"**Sounds of voices** reached my ears from behind me. They were shouting, 'Go to the temple. Go to the temple!' I heard rifle shots, and they seemed to close in around me. The fear within my mind created slow motion: people moving in the shadows, children crying.

"**Changing my direction** to go to the hidey-hole, I ran as fast as these legs could carry me. In darkness, with blurred and tear-filled eyes, in the cold night air, I ran. It was time to forego my family and friends. 'Be obedient through our love,' I could hear Uncle saying. 'Don't look back.'

"**Desperately** moving the *vine*-y top that covered the hole, in the distance I saw my best friend running with his sister, Flo. I froze as they ran past in the shadows. I wanted to call out to let them know where I was, where the hidey-hole was, where they would be safe. But, 'Nowhere is really safe.' I needed to hide, to be quiet, to cover the top and go deep into the hole. Oh no! I forgot the food and wine-water.

"**People were screaming**, the night seemed to go on forever, and I smelled gunpowder. My school friends were among those fleeing, even the bullies who teased me for carrying the lunch bucket filled with bean soup. It always spilled over as I ran through the woods trying not to be late for school. I feared being forced to write, a hundred times or more, the same old sentence. Our teacher-imposed repetition as a strong reminder. 'I will not be late.' Didn't work: I was late most of the time because of playing games.

"Running to this hidey-hole was not like running to school for fear of writing lines: I did not want to get shot. Almost the same type of fear was deep in my stomach. Fast and heavy heartbeats throbbed in my chest. Could the soldiers see me as I ran? Wondering if the bullets were near me, I ducked with every shot.

"Please God, let the bullets miss my friends. German orders were being shouted. The more the Nazis shouted, the more cries and moans did hang in the air. Auntie's clothes used to hang on a rope, blowing in the wind as they dried, and this occurred to me. With every shot came a flinch from my body, but I needed to make it to the little hole. It might save my life. Yet what would life be like without Auntie, without Uncle, without my friends?

"As I crawled into the hidey-hole I nested down deep, on one big root that stuck out of the dirt. Placing my hands over my ears didn't block out the cries and gunfire. Would these sounds ever stop? Could this just be a nightmare? Uncle coming to shake me, to wake me – smelling the breakfast, being time to get up for school. Instead the smell of wet dirt and roots told me this was not any night terror in a dream. I was in the hidey-hole and this terror was real. This night would turn into day and those memories will never go away.

"Uncle had instructed, 'Your time will come to help others. It's just not now. God deliver us from all evil.'

"Daybreak came with so much bright sunshine that it shone through the intertwining branches which hid the opening of the hole. The sun was warm on my face even though the dirt was still cold and damp. The smell of smoke and burnt wood filled the air and I could taste ash from whatever had burned in the night. Sometime during the night the cries had stopped as I slept. Now, dark images lingered from my dreams. The images hovered over the hole, haunting my thoughts. There were moans like at the Sunday-evening operas we used to attend in the outdoor theater of the ghetto. The tenors seemed to chase the scoundrels after they'd ransacked and killed. There was screeching, which conveyed doom with resounding, high-pitched voices. The air was now filled with stillness and haunting silence.

"As the sun's rays heated and warmed the ground which surrounded me, I climbed to the top, peeking out. I could not believe how the small green forest had changed. Fresh-smelling green pine needles had been replaced with burned wood. The landscape, once covering the ground with copper-colored carpet, was now smoky branches and ashes of withering leaves. So many branches missing. The forest, dead. Only the sunrays remained the same. Our gold- and rust-colored pine needle carpet, once a playground, was now an ashen floor graced by skeletons of fallen trees.

"As the evening shadows moved, the hunger pangs began with the memories of Auntie filling my knapsack with breads and cookies. The hunger sounds and throbs began with a little rumble and a lot of pain. Wanting bread melting in my mouth with wine-water instead of tasting smoke. I didn't know how long this hole would be my home.

"Although my stomach ached, thinking of games and stories helped keep my mind busy. I repeated names of my friends, Uncle's prayers, stories of Auntie's grandparents on the farm milking the cows and giving us warm milk with biscuits and jam. Near their little cottage farmhouse they picked berries from the forest. Memories of sitting at night by the hot stove now kept my mind busy. It was not easy to fall asleep while hearing the cries. The hidey-hole became darker as the sun set.

"I focused on grandparent stories and the crisp chill in the air. The distinct cries got louder but faded somewhat as I slept. All of this mixed with visions of my friends playing, hiding behind the large tree trunks, playing tag while running home from school.

"We had no forest, and there in the distance smoke filled the buildings of the ghetto. Parts of buildings were still standing, but we had no home. As the night ended and turned into day, the sparrows didn't sing. They too understood: we are all homeless."

Mama Jack

As if sitting in the swing on the porch in Louisiana, I contemplated. How much pain Noah's grandfather must have experienced in telling the story. We had all noticed his voice beginning to quiver, his sky-blue eyes turning to a deep gray – he was ready to end the story. Stillness filled the room, until the silence was broken by people making espresso, and mmm that coffee smell filled the air. People moved around and most headed to the kitchen for cake and a cup of coffee. Some went over to Noah's grandfather and talked quietly and in an Italian I couldn't follow.

The sun was starting to set. I looked around and, there in a corner, my host family was talking with Noah's father. They had entered during the storytelling. They looked tired so I grabbed my teaching bag and headed toward the door, thanking everyone and hugging a select few. On the drive home, thoughts of being in the hidey-hole – at night, waiting for the night terrors – filled my mind and heart. How sad he, the child, must have felt, fearing for the safety of family and friends. For him to see what happened to the little forest, so leafless and burned, along with his home . . . fearing everyone he loved to be gone like the trees. All of what resembled life was no more.

The next day at school, entering the building, I couldn't get the story of the forest out of my mind. The choir was practicing the Negro spiritual *For His Eyes are on the Sparrow.* Thinking of Noah's grandfather and the birds in the forest, my eyes began to water up. What timing. The music was endearing, similar to words the slaves had used, but different, changed accents on the gospel lyrics. It sounded like a totally different song from the way it was sung in Big Momma's church. Rich childhood memories of hot summer days in Louisiana, breeze and fish-smell from the nearby Mississippi River coming through the church windows, brought daydreams to me of where the slaves must have sat before the Slave Pastor preached. *Gimme that Old Tyme Religion*, believing in the Lord, they sang with memories of their kinfolk walking off those slave ships to be sold.

A slave coming from an island which held slaves for import, my great-great-great-grandmother raised Mama Jack. Some time after the Emancipation Proclamation, decades later, slaves in her Louisiana town were allowed to leave. They left with only small knapsacks of belongings and their lives. Most had to leave their children with former slaves who remained. Mama Jack would sit on the rocks by the church watching the steamboats travel the Mississippi River to and from New Orleans, wondering if her mother was onboard. Mama Jack, my great-grandmother, prayed to one day see the woman who birthed her, and who did not, could not, find her way back home.

I wondered if the sparrows in Grandfather's story would find their way back home. Struggling slaves kept faith, focused like the sparrows in the burnt forest, wanting to go home. Just as from the Egyptians, they wanted their freedom. Sparrows and slaves alike, watched over by the Lord, in hard times which will pass.

My voice is deep like my grandmother's, and church people say the voice is an "old soul." Rich in traditional tones, Negro spiritual tones, sometimes so deep I'd surprise myself singing high and low notes timed so close to each other. Mama Jack did say it was the spirit that filled me, hands of angels that guided my voice to move from lows to highs and to touch many old souls.

Chained slaves, I could see them walking down the plank of the ship, young men and women, no older than I was when I sang in morning church service. Big Momma often told me that story, but it was special when she <u>showed</u> me, from the small window in church, where the ships had traveled and the slaves had marched for buying and bidding. The song, *Home, I Wanna Go Home*, takes on meaning, expressing fear the slaves must have felt and the hopelessness they experienced.

Home, I Wanna Go Home

*Dere's no rain to wet you,
O yes I wanna go home.*

*Dere's no sun to burn you,
O yes I wanna go home.*

*O push along, Believers,
O yes I wanna go home.*

*Dere's no hard trials,
O yes I wanna go home.*

*Dere's no whips a-crackin',
O yes I wanna go home.*

*My brudder on de wayside,
O yes I wanna go home.*

*O push along, My Sis',
O yes I wanna go home.*

*Where dere's no stormy weather,
O yes I wanna go home.*

*Dere's no tribulation,
O yes I wanna go home.*

Songs like the one the Italian choir was singing had been handed down from generation to generation. With memories of their ancestors, the children of slaves built this little church on the banks overlooking where slaves had been forced to pick cotton, yet with songs of praise. God takes care of the birds; God will take care of our hearts. Music tells of dark times, like Noah's grandfather's story: waiting, hiding in a hole, anticipating the return of the sparrows.

As I walked down to the choir room, to sing or not to sing was a very emotional decision. Questionable to me was the potential quiver in my voice – my self-esteem was low. Would my voice hold up? Could I express the family history in this song? To walk into the choir room and to be greeted with smiles overcame my trepidation felt so deeply. Encouragement is good. Okay, this is a done deal.

After the choir completed their song the music teacher looked up from the piano. She was giving me my cue. There in the corner was Noah sitting on the stool ready to play. I said, "May I sing the song the way it was taught to me in my early years?"

And, so, with a nod from the music teacher, I sang with all my heart. The first few notes were hums and the last few notes brought tears. I was picturing the walk up the hill to church. I could hear the Louisiana choir singing, always starting with hums.

They said that was the way the slaves did it to clean the church of unwanted spirits, but it really was a signal that the coast was clear for those running toward freedom or hiding from the Master. Pack, get onboard. The Underground Railroad is ready to leave.

Get onboard little chil'in,
Get onboard little chil'in,
Get onboard little chil'in,
There's room for many aboard.

That song was the cue to get in the hole, where they'd stay till the coast was clear. The little one-room church was packed, and there was a hole under the church.

Noah played as if he knew the notes even before they left my mouth. Noah struck the chords which matched the tones of another student playing the cello. How amazingly their instruments did match the deepness in my voice.

These nostalgic notes formed tears in my eyes, thinking of Big Momma and Mama Jack, singing at sunset on the front porch as the breeze blew cool air from east of the Mississippi River. We were practicing for our Sunday solos. Big Momma brushed Mama Jack's silver hair and braided it into three equal sections like the splitting of harmony in our voices.

As I began to sing for the class, I envisioned the Colored Cemetery where slaves were buried behind the church. Deeply I felt the words. There was a hush of silence throughout the room.

Go down, Moses, way down to Egypt-land,
And tell old Pharaoh to let my people go.

The song took on a depth of feeling which I hadn't felt since childhood. We needed an uplifting in that Italian music room, and the rhythm took on a different atmosphere. We ended the song with clapping and singing. *Let my People Go* just came out of the air. I was stunned to see children with tears in their eyes. Before they began clapping, you could have heard a pin drop. I thanked them as I walked quietly and softly out the choir-room door.

Grandfather

That evening everyone wanted Grandfather to continue his hidey-hole story. They sat straight up to listen.

"**Stones were piled** outside the hidey-hole to draw heat from the sun, for the cold night which would come early. The blanket that Auntie put into my knapsack was scratchy and not that warm, but I was grateful for her loving me enough to make me take it. I would put it in the hole for safekeeping. It was knitted the same as my sweaters, always the same stitch, always itchy.

"**My Auntie would sit** beside that black stove, telling stories of when she was a little girl. She'd knit something to be worn, and sometimes she'd look away as if dreaming then smile with a sigh. When the cries outside my hidey-hole started that night, I tried to think of her stories, counting how many times she'd told the same one.

"Tonight I could tell the cries were coming from the direction of the temple. There are people inside? Cries for help, rifle sounds, then an eerie silence.

"Were these real sounds of people or just made-up things in my head? No food, no water, not even a scratchy old knitted blanket to keep the people warm. And where did the shots come from?

"As the darkness set in and the shadows came across the branches and leaves that hid the hole, I fell asleep so deeply. When I woke up it was still dark. The birds didn't sing. I heard only sounds of people rushing through the woods and orders being called out: stay in line, children this way, adults move forward. I could not tell in what direction people were moving, but they were being ordered! I think they were going to the North Fields where the vineyards were planted but not harvested. There was very little in the North Fields but a small creek, some trees – but mostly just open field."

When the school bell rang, I was just singing the final lyrics. The music teacher got up from her piano and rushed over to me. She sort of startled me, and her smile told me that I had not messed up too badly. She was holding a book of papers – handed them to me, saying in a pleasant voice, "Please sing these songs for us tomorrow morning."

Homework?!?! Okay, homework! As this day went along and I proceeded to my classroom for teaching, I could hear in my mind the choir singing music the way I sang it. It was remarkable! They were learning soul-singing.

It was a girl playing the cello, and she and Noah added gospel rhythms to the songs. By the end of the day each class had practiced the new versions. There was no guessing about the plan to learn African-American spirituals. This was really becoming a different adventure, hearing students enunciate words and even add southern dialect the slaves sang, slurring words like *M-ohh-ses*. Southern-Louisiana dialect is so different from how people in other countries hear and pronounce words. A little bit of French did intertwine with Africans' voices which imitated the sound of drums, deep tones echoing their various dialects.

These students were of the impression everybody in the U.S.A. spoke the same homogenized American dialect. It took me some time to realize that many of them had never seen an African-American. In the lifetimes of these young students never had any Negro teacher crossed their threshold. Many Africans came from various regions to work in the vineyards but not one African-American, especially not one to sing gospel with blues-shifts and runs for students to learn.

That evening I walked my route around the town and along the paths which somehow led me to Noah's home. I began to look over my homework papers while I walked. They were handwritten music scores, most dating back to the 1940s during World War Two. The teacher must have believed I could play the piano, and could read. And to give me these original scores, she really trusted me.

I thought of Noah's father and the sitting room with the old piano, a room where all chairs and the sofa faced inward like a circle, and this was where Grandfather told his stories. So taking the sheets of music to Noah's father would give me a reason to visit and perhaps have an early dinner. My mind could taste the hot pasta with homemade sauce. *First* dinner then *second* dinner. I was now that committed to the Italian tradition of eating, like a worthy traveler, like a Hobbit: first dinner and second dinner with wine only during the second meal.

As the path turned I could see Noah's father was outside. Was he waiting for me? This habit of his was becoming known in the neighborhood, the way he looked at me and waited for me to pass their apartment. He was waiting for me, a gleam in his eyes. Noah's dad wanted me to stop by to visit before walking to the edge of town where my host family would pick me up. He'd drive me home just about every night now. I would start my walk from school in a haphazard direction but it seemed I'd somehow make it to Noah's apartment every time. This time I really needed help to read the music sheets.

Noah's father was a tall man with black hair and dark Italian features. His frame was thin but the most impressive thing about him was his smile. Oddly his teeth were sort of crooked and overlapped visibly in the front. My teeth overlapped on the bottom, so in my mind we matched. I don't know why I thought of such silly things as I neared their apartment, but there was the father standing on the stairs with this incredible grin, saying, "Pasta tonight?"

From the top window I could hear Noah saying, "We know it's your favorite." He was right. There was something about his father's homemade pasta that was so delightfully delicious. I never had the heart to tell him I did not like red sauce, but his sauce was different. Well, he did make it and it was not like the jars in the store my mother would use and add her own green and red peppers and onions.

The first time eating his pasta he had shown me how to use the spoon and fork. I confessed very early, as the steaming heap of pasta made its way to the table, that using a spoon and fork was not the way we ate in the inner city. He was so gracious to show me and that is the day he touched my hand. The feeling of a nice man and his smile was exhilarating. His eyes looked down at me. Blushing and glowing just went all over my face. Our eyes met for only a second but in that second there was a joy, peace and so much happiness.

As we walked up the stairs I handed him the papers and looked up, trying not to meet his eyes. "Do you think you would be able to help me sing some of these songs?" The words were from old spirituals but because the music for the song *Go Down Moses* was so different, I thought it safer to hear the songs played before singing.

"Of course," he said. "After dinner? I will call your family and let them know you will be a little later than normal and of course, driving you back would be an honor for me." Now the glow was all over my face and my heart. By this time my heart was beating outside my body. Very sure I was that he could read my transparent face, which brought on more blushing.

After dinner I washed and dried the dishes as Noah put them away. It was amazing what he could do despite being blind. In the school, in the challenged classrooms, everything centered on the students. It all began after the Second World War. The stories from the elders expressed how differently people in the town related to children and fostered their desire to ensure the town's survival. The challenged classroom had many different kinds of students. Most were blind, which was strange for me because American public schools had schools for children with sight challenges, but in Italy there were so many blind kids.

Noah's father spoke of his trips to America for treatments. Noah had a sponsor who took care of his medical expenses, a man who sang tenor, also blind, who had attended Noah's school. In fact, the first song he learned to play was the same song a certain woman teacher had taught both Noah and his sponsor. It was one of our African-American songs, *What a Wonderful World*.

On his piano Noah's father began to play the scores while we cleaned up after dinner. The sun had not yet started to set, and most of the people in the town ate rather late, so we had lots of time. As Noah's dad played an incredible flow of softness filled the air. These songs were spiritual but his timing was *not the same*. And songs without the runs were like gray holes needing to be filled.

Sometimes I Feel like a Motherless Child was the first song he played. When Noah began to strum, and then add, I began to hum and then to sing. I walked over to the open window and sang to the window. The breeze felt so good on my face. It was a long way from home and I missed my grandmother, the Mississippi River breeze, even the smell. So far from home for the first time ever. I missed seeing other Americans and being able to understand what was said, not to mention I really couldn't follow songs on the radio. I missed my TV shows spoken in English. There was nothing like <u>Sanford and Son</u> for me, because I knew their expressions.

"Do you know the history of this story?" I asked Noah as his father played. Noah shook his head no, his father turned toward me, and the story just came out of me. Mothers who had children, many fathered by white masters, would take their babies to the river and drown their own children rather than give them a life of slavery. Yearning for Africa they wanted to go home. With remorse for their lost children, they longed to go home.

I sang the song again without the music so that Noah and his father could hear the deepness in this song. It was more than just notes. The runs and the notes held emotion. The meaning of the song gave the spirit a freedom to roam in my heart, being a long way from home.

*   *   *

There were kids' bikes all over the grass, plus many older people coming and going, the next day when I got to school. As I approached the music room, I was surprised to see Noah's father. He greeted me with that incredible smile and wide, sort-of-hazel eyes which changed colors with the clothes he wore. He always greeted me *Buon giorno*, making my heart throb. He went directly to the piano and began to play, so passionately, the melody of *A Long Way from Home*.

There was a hush and all eyes were on me. I looked around the room packed with students, parents and grand- and great-grandparents. Thinking I could sneak to the back of the room – but this did not happen. Before getting to the middle of the room the Music teacher called my name. With a wave of her hand she motioned for me to come to the front. Only a <u>few</u> songs had we practiced the night before. The choir students began walking to the risers along the sides of the room. So, a music presentation was why all these parents had come? Or, not?

The teacher began to direct them with hums as Noah's father commenced playing. The cello, a violin, and Noah on his guitar began the prelude to *Go Down Moses*. The baritones and tenors had such beautiful parts and the quality of the hums was breathtaking. When the teacher pointed to me, words and tones from my Big-Momma memories just came out flowing. Without any rehearsing, music just came out. Harmony blended just right, runs were perfect, exactly the way we'd practiced in class on the previous day of school. When I sang, "do believe," it was with a high but melodic voice. There was no music, just my voice. The choir hummed as we ended the song with my words . . . and with my tears.

Noah's father began to play *Sometimes I Feel like a Motherless Child, a Long Way from Home*. I started very soft, still full of emotion from the previous song, but strong and deep. In this song the range of my voice could be heard and felt. This song reminded me of Mama Jack sitting by the river watching the ferries and steamboats at the slave-auction port, and wondering if her mother would ever come home. With no memory of her mother, Mama Jack would look for facial features like her own.

To my surprise the choir was right on key. They swayed in a rhythmic tempo. When the director-teacher looked at me, I knew it was my cue. I looked around the room and my comfort was in the contact I made with the eyes. Noah's father played so magnificently. How could my voice equal his playing and the choir? Seeing Noah, searching for my sound, I began to sing.

The flow of music filled the air. It was easy for me to slide an octave to the high notes, plus change to another key. I followed Noah's lead and sang my notes as if I carried a precious child in my arms. What an incredible surprise: the crispness and ease of each note sung, the choir echoing each verse. Even the cello had a part that surprised me.

The song and music were beautiful and I thanked God for allowing me to use my voice to sing His praise. As I sang I thought of what it was like to give up a child for freedom. I felt for the children given up in those slavery times, mothers leaving their babies and their older children, as they fled to the North, an unknown land. The lyrics began:

Thank you Lord for saving my soul,
Thank you Lord for making me whole,
Thank you Lord for giving to me,
Thy greatest salvation, so rich and so free.

Ahh long way from home,
Ahh long way from home.
Sometimes I feel like a
Motherless child ahh long way from home.

That evening, after school, as I walked toward Noah's house, which was becoming a regular route,

I noticed many people in the windows as if waiting for me. There was a crowd in front of the little apartment building and, yes, Noah's father was standing on his favorite stair. I was still walking up to the apartment when he announced, "The Elder has a story for you tonight, Bella Bea Bella, one that he has not told for a long time. In the 1940s, at war, these townspeople heard the colored soldiers sing your way, with feeling in the rhythm. The story is about the children going home."

The Temple

"The hidey-hole was starting to warm up or I was getting used to the cold. My legs were starting to cramp up and I really needed to walk. When the sun set I crawled out of the hole. The crying had just about stopped but the rifle fire continued.

"As I walked through the bushes I could not believe my eyes. It looked like dancing shadows – my eyes were playing tricks with the sun through the saplings. There at the edge of the forest was the temple all boarded up. Instead of stained-glass windows that reflected the sun, I saw dark shadows on wood that covered the glass. Where did all the people go, the ones who would run to the temple to pray, seeking protection from the Germans? Did they sneak out during the night? Or were they still inside?

"As I came closer to the temple it became apparent there were many German soldiers, rifles on their backs, walking the grounds with large dogs. 'Please God, don't let them sniff me out,' I prayed, as they walked toward the opening at the back of the temple. This felt like I was in a gray night-dream.

"There was a little window my friends and I would crawl through when Uncle and the men held special meetings. How else could we know what was going on? Listening to Auntie and the women just didn't work – wrong information. They would only talk about each other. Uncle's group talked about the happenings in other towns near us and how our townspeople planned to help them. We kids didn't care about babies being born or how to make tiramisu pudding and beef stews. From Uncle's group we'd hear plans of survival if the train were to stop in our town. Did they suspect our town might be next? Or perhaps they did envision the building, in our town, of the last concentration camps of the war. The men often said our nearness to Austria and proximity to the train tracks would make us the final town. Was our end really near, or had we missed the phenomenon of concentration camps? My mind raced with thoughts, 'Please God, let the little window still be open so that I can crawl inside.'

"**Sure enough** the window was not boarded. Behind the bushes the window was just the way we left it the last time we kids met to eavesdrop on the men. That was always more enlightening than listening to recipes for soup.

"**As I crawled** into the little window, being careful not to make any noise or break the glass, the smell of rotten meat not only surprised me, but I felt dizzy and ill. To my surprise, the stomach I thought was empty gave way. Everything I did not know I had eaten, and what I wanted to have eaten, was hurled out of my mouth with such great force I didn't have time to turn, it just came straight out. My legs gave way. As I fell to the ground there was Seth, my best friend, with his eyes open. Normally we did everything together except for that night the train stopped. That had been a week ago, when he went to the temple with his mom and two sisters, instead of coming into the hidey-hole with me."

Porgy and Bess

Before I left school the choir director came to my classroom. She looked so serious, I wondered if

I had not sung well enough or perhaps I'd moved a little much with my eyes closed feeling the music – well, the choir had swayed.

She looked at me with glazed eyes and asked if I would sing the next night in the meeting hall. Mmmm, this seemed okay. There were not many people in the town, so . . . a town meeting, right, this was alright. I was thinking perhaps the choir would often perform during breaks when business in town was slow. It was not harvest time and everyone seemed to be alright with things. Not too much bicycle traffic, the town only had one stoplight, and singing in such a setting really worked for me. Cows were crossing the streets near the train tracks, so, everything seemed normal, so, yes to singing at the town-hall meeting.

I left school. As I walked my favorite route I thought about the songs in Big Momma's church. Every Sunday there were selected songs that connected, giving inspiration, with what Pastor Seabrook would preach about. One of my favorites was the one about the Straw-ta-berries. He was comparing life to how they grew. I don't remember much about the scripture, but the way he pronounced "strawberries" I will never forget.

Big Momma sang *Summertime*, her deep voice so moving. Then she would say, "Theyz just off de vigh-ine, theyz just cost de dime; mmmm straw-ta-berries . . ." on a high pitch, and then, "straw-ta-berries" at a middle pitch. Big Momma would say it as if she were the strawberry lady selling door-to-door down her road. What I liked even better, she'd sing the same song, as written, from the musical *Porgy and Bess*, and it was beautiful to listen to her voice. It was Louisiana-hot in her church. Women had their eyes closed, fans keeping time with all the music sung, that last Sunday before I'd return home to Chicago, the last Sunday in July in that particular summer of my childhood.

The route past Noah's house was long, so there was lots of time to think. Seeing his father on the steps now almost every day brought such a smile to my face and put a glow in my heart. I wanted not to smile but that just didn't work. When I saw him, my heart would race and a certain feeling of joy would take over my entire body. He'd created a new experience for me, far deeper happiness than I ever could imagine. I wondered if he felt what I felt. He was very tall, at least nine inches taller than me, and his eyes were as blue as the sky when the sun hit them just in the right spot. He had a dimple in his chin that grew deeper when he smiled, and his eyes would smile at me, turning a deep silvery blue-green when our eyes met.

Our eyes did not meet very often because I did everything possible to avoid it. The smile of happiness would just appear on my face and blushing and glowing became apparent under my cocoa-brown skin.

Thinking I liked this man, there were some complications, however. His wife's picture all over the apartment. Noah was blind. How could those pictures be for Noah? One thing I had learned from Big Momma was not to "read more into things." He was different from anyone I'd ever known, and not just his looks or the incredible way he spoke English. I wondered if he knew how my heart felt about him.

When he saw me that dimple in his chin got really deep. He did not smile as much as I did. It seemed he could control his face, yet the deepness in that dimple was a sure giveaway. "Your voice is as beautiful as you," he would say. Wow, my heart is now his and he didn't have to ask for it. It's a good thing he doesn't know it, at least not now. As we walked up the stairs I felt him directing me by touching my back. Well, that was a little different – he had never directed me before. Noah sat by the window, feeling the breeze on his face. You would not know he was blind. He rarely wore dark glasses, but he'd turn his head toward sounds . . .

except when he sat by the window as if waiting to see someone walk down the twisted road.

Sometimes I would stop to get flowers and sometimes bread or bread pudding from the shops. Today I picked up chocolates because I knew this was Noah's favorite and it would add time after dinner for us to sit, eat *cioccolata*, and talk about the day. I did not always stay for dinner, although I was always asked, with an offer for Noah's dad to take me home a little later. Today I wanted to stay mostly because, well . . . Noah's father played piano for me in school, but I sought his company. Absence is not a good thing when it tugs at your heart. I wanted to find a way not to miss him and to keep his smile, with the deep dimple in that chin, out of my mind. I needed to focus on schoolwork.

As we walked out to the stairs to wait for my host family to pick me up, he touched my hand. "I want to tell you something. It is important," he said. "The pictures of my wife are all over the apartment because I did not want Noah to forget his mom. Although he cannot see, he knows the frames are there and every day he waits for her to return. The songs you sing have a different meaning for everyone and when you sing, our two hearts touch in some way. Today when playing for you I could feel you even deeper than I could expect. Your eyes were closed so you didn't see me, but I could not keep my eyes off you. You are so beautiful to me."

It was the way he said "beautiful" that made my heart jump and it had been jumping a lot those past few days. His eyes sparkled against his black, straight hair blowing in the breeze. I was speechless. Amazingly Noah was playing *You are so Beautiful to Me* on his electric guitar. The strings sounded like a person singing, so I sang, "You are everything I hoped for, you are everything to me." Then his father joined me singing, "You are so beautiful to me."

Could this really be happening? Just like a love story? In Italy, on these stairs, looking at a man I liked who liked me back. It was just too much. Yes, one tear rolled down my cheek. He took his thumb and, with so much gentleness, he wiped it away. The tear was probably due to the wind and my allergies but what a moment in time. He liked me and I liked him back. Imagine liking someone through just a smile, and we had a favorite song, which I thought about, all the way back to the host family home.

Grandfather

"Walking over the bodies of people was so difficult. I didn't want to look down but needed to know where I was stepping. I kept thinking, 'It's not real. This is a night-terror dream. Just keep walking.' But where was I walking? I found myself walking up the winding staircase where the rabbi would prepare for temple. All of his books still were on the wall's bookcase. It was quiet there. Peaceful. The window was not boarded and you could look across to where the vineyards ended and see the tall grass, and there, right where the vineyards stopped, you could see the railroad tracks.

"**Long buildings** were getting erected, some type of long house, as if for many people. I could see the shadow of the bakery's deliveryman. Uncle did say, 'That gent is as strong as an ox.' He was carrying something on his back. Instead of delivering cakes, he was taking bricks and large pieces of wood to men and women building long houses. In a series of rows, with silvery blue-green barbwire fences, these buildings replaced beautiful vineyards. There was one small house in the center where soldiers were stationed. It all resembled a summer camp for kids and, there in the middle, a flag was waving in the night breeze. I began to understand the camps Uncle talked about when we'd sit around the stove at night. The *symbol* was in the middle of the waving flag. Oh no, they were building a camp for the people from the ghetto.

Uncle and Auntie, were they at home? Was this the camp they talked about when we sat by the black stove?

"I sat at the window until the sun started to rise. The buildings were almost complete – then the cries began. Little ones at first, but then so many, cries and moans, louder every second. I covered my ears trying to block out the sound, but it didn't work. I knew I needed to get to the hidey-hole before light or I would have to stay in the temple, with the bodies of everyone I'd known for as long as I'd been in this small town. The stench had become weaker to my nose, less noticeable with time, but I knew it was time to get back to the hidey-hole.

"I found my way to the small window and crawled out, covering the window with branches, twigs and leaves. I decided just to look where the sounds were coming from, although I had already seen the goings-on from the top of the staircase, from the rabbi's room. 'Halt! Who goes there?' was the cry and I just froze. I think it must have been an angel who rustled the nearby leaves because the soldiers took off running, chasing the wind. I was scared. I almost wet my pants, which I did at night around this time anyway, but I did not want to sleep wet in the cold smelling like my own waste. I ran as fast as I could, yet I needed a place to relieve myself. Yes, they ran after the wind. As Uncle would say, 'God loves and protects us.'

"**As I ran back** to the hidey-hole I could not get out of my head the sight of the window that had no pane. The cries echoed in my ears and blended with sounds from this new camp. As I ran and looked back I discovered there were two different camps. I needed to know, so I ran toward the sounds, and at this point there was no caring about my own life. Uncle, Auntie and the people of the town, were they safe? Were they like the people in the temple who cried before dying? Was this the pattern before that kind of death?

"**As I turned,** running between trees, I saw Emily, my best friend's sister, in the window. It looked as if she was holding their baby sister. Emily was crying out, 'She is dead.' That was enough to bring me to my knees. How much more, God, how much more can my heart take? Will they all be gone when this night terror is over?"

*   *   *

The chatter in the school was joyful, full of life, and it was three nights before the town-hall meeting. One of the teachers in the teacher copyroom, their workroom, began to talk about the Stalin Group. I had not heard that name since my freshman year in high school. Was this the same Stalin? Perhaps many of the townspeople would go to the Stalin Group, not to the town meeting where I was to sing. That would reduce the number of people . . . and why did the number of people bother me? Just relax. Breathe three deep breaths. That always worked. Mmm, three times breathing deep works.

Going to Noah's home to rehearse I walked very slowly knowing I needed to go over the songs. I could not make up my mind which song I would share with the town. But my feelings were more of safe-emotion, knowing Noah's father would be there on the stairs waiting to walk me up to the flat. Maybe this is a tradition. Why do Italian men always seem to wait for women on the stairs to walk them up? I didn't care why. I just knew my heart was jumping, my legs trembling, knowing how distracted I was at thoughts of this man, the first ever to touch my heart and mind in this way. He would be on the stairs waiting for me.

We went up, to await my host family. My heartbeat was so fast and the excitement was just so overwhelming. I wondered if Noah's father knew these feelings were new, different and very welcome in my life. Ever since Big Momma's passing there had been a gray part in the center of my heart. Being with Noah and his father was filling that emptiness. Thinking _family_ was what my heart missed, the host family was great. It was like being a part of a family that was not mine. But, with Noah and his father it was like they were _my_ family.

After Noah's father closed the door, slowly we walked down the stairs and I could feel his hand touch my back. My body did something very strange. Instead of moving away it went closer to his hand. I turned, looking up at him, his eyes steel-gray blue. He bent down and our lips touched just for a brief second . . . so very gentle. It was like one of those butterfly kisses from Big Momma. She would come into my bedroom to kiss me, thinking I was asleep, and her eyelashes would touch my skin. Only instead, this kiss was not on my forehead.

When we got to the bottom of the stairs I slid my hand into his hand. He squeezed it gently, then turned and kissed me again, only this time it was longer but just as tender. He likes me and I like him back!

That night my prayer was very different. I prayed in song, using a soft voice not to wake up little Stefano. The six-year-old slept in the bedroom next to mine with his dog Molly, either on the floor or in his bed. I looked out the window, up to the heavens, sky blue mingling with royal blue . . . lavender, pinks, colors of clouds mixing with an orange sunset.

Incredible evening – the man of steel-gray blue eyes. My heart beat so fast as I yearned to go home and smell Mama Jack's rose perfume and to hear Big Momma's hums of praise – praying in song. The *Thank You* song was my favorite. The pastor often asked me to solo on Children's Day when children acted in the roles of adults, like collecting the offering. Practicing with Noah, how I wished I'd thought to suggest the *Thank You* song. Perhaps we could try this song tomorrow. Noah was good at hearing the melody, playing and adding his own string arrangements. After hearing songs he could simply play them: the same way, not changing a chord, and embellishing. Falling to sleep, I set myself to singing:

My faith cannot be broken,
for I believe in you.
I will trust You Father forever,
I know Your love is true.
No one can make me doubt You,
no one can ever pull our love apart.
For I have faith in You Father,
and the love that's in my heart.

Thank You Father
for the love you send my way.

Thank You Father
for the beauty of this day.

Thank You Father
for the love you send to me.
For faith, joy and peace
and blessings giv'n to me.

Sleep came easily to me that night and my heart felt so complete. Noah and his father were now a part of my family, so I included them when asking God to protect and bless my family. God knew what was going on inside me and I had faith in God as my center.

The Camp

"Snuggling with that scratchy blanket was so welcome in the hidey-hole. As I closed my eyes I could see my friend Seth lying on his side. It was like the way he looked sleeping, after we laughed and talked during sleep-over nights at my house. I could not, will not, forget his eyes so still, like glass, so empty. Sometimes at the end of the week Auntie would let me have a sleep-over. We would all lie on the floor around the black stove. Burning logs warmed us, as we laughed ourselves to sleep. I was now hearing Uncle's favorite line so loudly in my head, 'You boys go to sleep!' We would even giggle about that as we continued to tell each other stories under the blankets. These were stories that were not true. We listened to each other anyway, pretending to believe every word. It was hard to think of Seth gone. It was even more terrifying to think of him on the temple floor, not buried. It was so hurtful not being able to lift him, pass his body through that window, bury him in the forest – even more painful than seeing his lifeless eyes.

"**In my dreams,** there in the hidey-hole, it was wonderful to hear Auntie calling me to breakfast and handing me my lunch pail as I ran out the door for school. The excitement of helping Uncle carry in wood after school for a few coins to go and buy candy from the store, mingled with other memories of the past. I began to fall in and out of sleep until the cries of the children started. They were moans while others were screeches. I could hear cries from small babies as I thought of Seth's sister standing in the opening of one of the newly built barracks holding their baby sister. There were also moans of adults, mostly sounds of women crying, 'Please let the children go. Feed the children.' Then rifle shots covered up the cries but did not stop the crying of babies. Screeches and moans filled my head with unseen horrors."

I needed to say something of Grandfather's stories in tomorrow's meeting. There was disgust on his face as he told his stories with tear-filled eyes, speaking the Italian words to say soldiers, heroes and cowards. Weren't these Nazis truly cowards persecuting old men like his Uncle and Auntie, women and children? The little boy wanted to be a hero and save them, but he felt like a coward in a hidey-hole trying to save himself. He was no longer thinking of himself but praying for the answer of how to save the others.

*   *   *

Teaching was a true love and this practice-teaching was not like working. My first teaching experience began at age ten as the Sunday-school teacher for a pre-school class. My Big Momma was amazed how I could handle the four-year-olds. Keeping them quiet with Mama Jack's sugar pops which she had freshly made on Saturday, I, the ten-year-old, would sing and tell stories. Even the pastor would stop by and sit for a while in my class and help me through the Bible story his wife had selected for me to teach. I would spend time during the week making and drawing characters on the Bible cards for my class to color. Each child had an individual card with three sentences and a drawing about the story. I would read the card aloud and the kids would talk about what kind of pictures they could draw and add to the scene. The Activity followed, singing a song about the story in a tune they knew. The Birthday Song was their favorite so most of the songs had that tune. Then we would hang their pictures up until their parents came. Each child would show a parent a picture on the wall and take it down to carry home. Every week we created a different story, lyrics or picture. Sometimes we'd create a dance or dress up as Bible characters which depended on how many old dresses I could come up with to cut up. Those days of playing teacher became the passion I now held so deeply. Noah and his father, through music, became a part of my heart. My thoughts drifted often toward them, and that was so much of my day.

Life had settled down and the students began to speak to me in English, correcting each other, and teaching me Italian. I was a part of their family now and in this little town everyone looked after each other. It was astounding how they began to understand mathematics as the language of science and how the process is science. They recognized that science words were a universal language. Most of the words came from their part of the world. Everything in Italy is old, with oak doors, handmade kitchen cabinets, even armoires where they stored Great-grandmother's wedding gown. Everything seemed to predate even the Founding Fathers of the United States, my country.

As I walked to Noah's house I could hear the afternoon birds singing. It was some type of finch, so tiny to have such a strong, high-pitched tune. Just to walk was great, to feel the breeze and greet every shopkeeper as I passed the shop. The unleavened bread smelled like sourdough and yeast mixing. The sun was warm but not hot, yet it heated the oils in my hair. The breeze was just enough to rearrange my hairstyle that took so long to design. Then I could easily brush it back with my hands, not disturbing the roller-set curls that defined a braid pattern. Did God mean for these feelings of ego to establish self-worth in my life? Never did I care for the design of my own hair. Big Momma didn't have many mirrors in the house and primping, as she called it, was not a good thing in our females-only home. Big Momma was so large and Mama Jack so petite, and I was their little girl who had characteristics from both. Big Momma was over six feet tall and Mama Jack was closer to five feet and there I stood at five feet four inches, with the slimness of my great-grandmother and the dark brown skin of Big Momma. They would call me their Sugar Baby because I did have the coloring of the medium-brown Sugar Baby candies. So primping in the mirror was not allowed in our house. We were three good-looking women: intelligent, hardworking, Christian women of color. I remember the affirmations and blessings they'd pray for me every morning. These were prayers asking for me to respect wisdom, to push away ego, and to allow God's intent for Sugar Baby's life to come to fruition. When my teenage years came those affirmations really helped, as the pimples came out all over my face and I grew two more inches, making me taller than any boy in my class.

Building the Camp

"**That next night** as I walked quietly toward the camp, I didn't need to hear the cries of the children to know the direction. Approaching that spot where I hid, I noticed the men who had built the small cabin for the soldiers were digging a ditch along the side of the camp. What if I also dug a way to get to that, connecting to that side of the camp? Could I use my ditch as a way to help other people escape? Was this God's answer to my prayers? Would it be possible for me to connect that ditch to my hidey-hole?

"**And then I saw** Seth's sister walking toward the soldiers with what looked like a soup pot. The soldiers held bowls out as she poured soup, while the children began to beg for food behind the barbwire fence. Her tears made my heart hurt so real and deep. If only I could help. If only I could get her and the baby out. I owed Seth that much. Yes, I wanted to get them all, but maybe-just-maybe I would be able to help her and the baby.

"**All I could think** about, walking back in the shadows of those trees, was how to dig and connect somehow to my hidey-hole. I had scouted out the direction and the way they calculated by pacing. I counted and imitated their paces from the barracks to the ditch. Could that be a way for me to know how to measure my ditch to the wire fence?

"**Remembering where** the tools were kept in the temple, I could . . . . That would mean I'd need to go back where Seth was lying. Seth's body was near the closet door where the tools were kept. I would need to move Seth to get into that closet. Perhaps that's where he had been crawling before he . . . . So many things were drifting in and out of my thoughts, filling my mind with visions. How could I help, or how would they catch me? The choice of what to do was overwhelming. That night, sleep was welcome until the dreams sought me and caught me with terror.

"**The following night,** my task was clear. I needed the tools before any work could be done and I needed a place to keep them tucked away during the day. Moving Seth's body was the first step, opening the door to the closet, not being sure if the tools were still in there. Perhaps the soldiers, forcing my uncle and the other prisoners to work, had moved the tools also.

"**I was now used to moving** in the dark. I turned my head in every direction. As I scurried toward the temple, I had happy memories of walking there in daylight. Now panic guided my steps as I walked in the twilight making sure I was not noticed by rifle-carrying soldiers. I looked for the bushes which covered that small window to the lower level of the temple. Threatening footsteps of solders, rustling leaves, my heart pounding so fast, so loud, with fear of being captured . . . I froze. The soldiers and the dogs were coming my way. I heard a loud voice in my head, 'Move,' so I began to run to the window buried in leaves.

"**The dogs growled,** so fearing the worst I picked up speed, not caring if they heard my footsteps. I would not give up. They would have to catch me throwing those bushes to the side. I dove into the half-open window expecting to fall on top of Seth's body. This fall would have been so unlike us rolling on the floor in front of that black stove while playing during a sleep-over. It would be so unlike us rolling in the schoolyard in the dirt during our mid-morning school breaks. I was simply not sure what the fall would be like, other than being unexpected, a hard landing of bump, a thump and a bounce on the hard floor.

"**To my disbelief,** Seth's body was gone and so were all the others. Because the temple had been so full of bodies, the smell still lingered. As the foot patrol approached the window I was sure one Nazi saw me. I was standing frozen with my mouth open. Perhaps he thought I was a ghost because he turned the dogs and went in the opposite direction. I would find my direction thanks to moss which clung to the same side of the trees. Nazis did not seem to have an interest in patrolling inside the temple or the grounds around it. I went to the closet and yes, the tools were there. Now, how to get them to the hidey-hole without the dogs sniffing out the way to my improvised home?

"**Up until this time** I really never thought about faith. Never had a reason to believe in the words of the adults. But now as I found my way back to where I felt safe, I thought about the teachings in the temple, the ark of Noah: faith and trust. Noah's world was mist without rain, and he trusted God to bring rain, then to float him on the flood and find land he had never seen. It is good to remember the past, to believe, to have faith. Uncle's words echoed in my ears. Faith, the faith I had in myself to accomplish things with God's hand guiding my every step. I needed a shovel. In opening the closet door I found that shovel with the handle Seth and I broke while playing in the coal pile.

"I could hear the rabbi's voice warning us to be careful. When the shovel broke I can remember how he looked at us with his raised eyebrow. Now I made my way back to the hidey-hole with the blade half of the shovel. But this was just what I needed to start digging the tunnel to the camp."

The aroma of coffee filled the room where we were hanging on every word, and the bread pudding was being placed on the table in small plates. It was time for a break. People talked their way to the table as the aroma replaced the tension of storytelling in the air. Noah asked me, "At the town meeting, will you please sing *It's a Wonderful World*?"

"Of course, Noah," I said, as we took our bread pudding back to our seats. I placed my coffee on the table by the sofa, both pieces of furniture older than my grandmother.

*   *   *

Grandfather :

"That day in the hole I imagined where to start the digging to rescue Seth's sister and the little baby. I could take the extra dirt out each night in the sack Uncle had placed in our hidey-hole with things he felt would help me survive cold nights. Using yarn from my blanket I could make strong rope and connect it to the branches that circled the nest of grass. I could use these things to make a pulley so that I could manage the weight of earth dug up. I'd pull up the sack to the tree line, where I could then cover it with the leaves, pine cones and needles. This was a workable plan.

"**After returning** from the temple that night with tools, after storing them safely within the roots, it was sunset as I headed toward the camp to lay out, in my head, where to end the digging. The closer I came to the camp the louder I heard the cries of children.

"**As those** cries became whimpers, I noticed Sarah, Seth's sister, standing in the window as if in a picture framed, holding her baby sister. Now hushed cries were so much more earthshaking than loud cries. After focusing on her for a moment, Sarah disappeared as in a dream. As my eyes wandered through the darkness, searching for her shadow... I remembered her carrying that soup pot to the solders. Seth's sister would certainly have a job which didn't call for building or construction work. She looked so small, her body, frail, just like others I had seen from a distance. It had not been long since the night the train stopped, but they all appeared so frail, so frightened. Yet solders looked healthier."

The Meeting

The next day in school was so long. My stomach was in my throat and full of nerves. That evening I was to sing while Noah would play. Students passed with smiles and teachers patted my back, saying, in Italian, "It will be an incredible night." Everyone seemed so excited about the night. They must have been talking about that other meeting; surely all would go to the Town Meeting and miss my singing.

After school, Noah came to my classroom. "Will you sing the first song my music teacher taught me?"

"Of course," I said, "but I may not know the words. Will you teach me?"

"Yes," he said with a huge smile as he unstrapped his guitar from behind his back. He found the stool where I generally sat while teaching the class. He began to play *What a Wonderful World.* Although I knew the tune I really never had known the words, so I hummed. I was saying to myself that I really needed to look up these words just as Noah said, "I'll teach you." He said the words just before I would sing them, and yes, this made it a wonderful world. "I will walk with you home," he said. "My father will meet us there."

These words touched my heart: thoughts of "us" and "home." I loved this young man and his father. My heart no longer did flips but this gentle happiness penetrated the inner core of my soul. How could a feeling be so gentle and yet so deep? How could just a smile from this child convey so much warmth of family and my small part of something larger? There was something special about sharing my inner being with these Italians.

I walked with Noah. He took the back of my arm, showing me how to lead him, as we walked the path to his apartment. Shopkeepers were outside. The baker had warm bread with a bottle of fresh-made olive oil. The town florist had a scented bouquet. At the wine-and-cheese *galleria* there was a large basket with plenty of room as if they knew we'd need room to carry all the good things others had for us.

"Noah, what's going on? Do you know why they call me *Bella Bea Bella* every time I pass their shops?" They were calling me beautiful – that I knew, in Italian – because they called me that all the time. Today there was something different in their voices, the way the words came out, and their eyes told a story. On this day, so many people stopped on the street in the square. People sat on benches facing the inner walkway and the fountain. Each time they'd call out *Bella Bea Bella* it was important to me to thank God, and them, thanking each person after saying hello.

I knew Mama Jack and Big Momma were smiling down on me from heaven because I could hear their voices in my head, "Be gracious. Smile, and stand up straight as you thank them."

I was very grateful for the blessings these townspeople had shown me. Blessings of caring, blessings of acceptance. I was overcome with the joy of knowing Noah, his father, his grandfather and everyone in town. Overcome, I began to sing:

Thank you God for saving my soul.
Thank you God for making me whole.
Thank you God for giving to me
Thy greatest salvation, so rich and so free.

Noah began to sing with me and I smiled so wide because now I realized why he never sang: His playing made up for the froggy sounds of his voice. He was definitely his father's son, to show kindness through his eyes and to show gratitude for just knowing somebody. His kindness touched the hearts of all who heard him.

As we approached the apartment, Noah's father was standing on his usual stair. He began to walk toward us with the biggest grin, showing those bright, crooked teeth. You could feel the happiness, the joy coming from his heart. He cared for me and this radiant smile was endearing. His eyes said *happy to see us*. He was really happy to see us walking home together from school.

"They are all waiting for you, Bea," he said as we walked closer, "waiting for you to hear Grandfather."

I didn't know what was expected of me. But I was ready to sing. Maybe it was time to listen and not sing. Either way, this fear-to-hear-the-train-stop story was becoming ours, not just theirs.

The Tunnel

"**To dig a tunnel** with the tunnel beginning inside my hidey-hole was a good idea, just in case I got discovered. When the night came, I began to take out the dirt. It'd been collected and put into the knapsack. Planning for night gave me something to think about during the day. I crawled, I dug this tunnel just big enough for me to squeeze through. I decided it'd be a good idea to dig, then make it larger, in case there were others in the woods needing a place a hide.

"**How could I tell** if I was going toward the camp or toward the temple? One faced sunrise, the other, sunset, but in this hole everything faced darkness. Different directions? Fear of digging in the wrong direction. Could I make a needle compass? I remembered a teacher taught us how to make a needle compass, and everything I needed was in that knapsack. Auntie packed it for me. The needle, the magnet, marbles and steel bearings in a tin can. Auntie packed all this for me to play with: to pick up things, to keep my mind busy. So a compass would be easy to make.

"**Praying the magnet** would work, I climbed to the top. I touched the moss on the side of a tree to see if I had a true north and YES it worked. I was ready now to dig with assurance I would not go in circles or toward the temple.

"**Days passed.** In my mind I visited the little camp the soldiers forced the people to make, and with every thought I dug faster and faster. The digging became more intense as I pictured Flo, my best friend's sister, holding her baby sister. Her eyes were so brown, so wide. Many times, in real life, I hid behind a tree and followed her movements through the camp. She cooked soup in big black pots on the fire, pouring some, then carrying soup to the soldiers. Watching her hold and rock the baby near the window, so many nights, her eyes wide and sad. Sometimes I imagined she could see me standing there behind the tree.

"**On the third night** of digging, I could hear water splashing against something. I knew I was near the trench, filled with water from the underground spring, where people went to carry water to wash the soldiers' clothes. This spring supplied water to the vineyards and to the fountain in the center of town. The townspeople still came to the spring during the day, but there was curfew about sunset. Everyone stayed in their homes.

"**As I dug closer** to the camp I could hear the rush of water was louder till I broke through and I felt cold, muddy water oozing into my crawlspace. The air was stale and smelled of human waste. As I crawled out of the tunnel I could see Flo standing in that window holding her sister. The baby was no longer crying and Flo wasn't shaking the small bundle of cloth either.

"**As** Flo looked up, she stopped in alarm. She could see me looking at her as I hid behind a half-burned tree. I ran to the hole with fear the soldiers might see me, yet they never had before. In the hole, with the half-handled, root-shaped shovel, I waved. I wanted to signal to her that I was not a dream.

"**Crawling through** the mud, over to the other side, I began to dig in some soft dirt. If only I could dig under the wire fence deep enough . . . perhaps she could climb out the window and into the hole. She saw me digging, and it worked. I was now facing her and the baby. With Superman strength, and I don't know where it came from, I pushed mud, I packed mud, to each side, widening the tunnel. When I looked up, Flo was gone from the window. Then she appeared on the side of the building, the baby wrapped tightly in linen just like Auntie's knapsack. When I reached her, we didn't speak. She crawled under the barbwire, handing me the baby, and we ran to the hidey-hole. As I went under I turned for the baby. And when I touched the bundle, that's when I realized the baby didn't move.

"Stiff, dead. I helped Flo through the fence and I motioned to the hole.

"She took the shovel and began."

Dear Reader, the sadness in the words "stiff" and "dead" almost overwhelm me, so let's bring this to a close. Our "Miss Bea" hopes you've adapted these stories to your own world. God gave us strong power of imagination, so "elders" of your own life fit right in.

To stitch up a few dangling threads of the storyline, indeed my performance at that meeting went fine, notwithstanding one drunk pianist. Noah married. And through song, the soldiers who buried Holocaust children get honored each year. The songs? Negro spirituals, the legacy left by black soldiers in that flag-stop Italian town. We don't have any life-or-death updates on the Italian heartthrob of Miss Bea, but perhaps it's better that way. The two never drove off into the sunset together — well, yes, perhaps in that *Wonderful World* of their minds, they did.

Made in the USA
Columbia, SC
02 June 2025